The ABSTRACT

Bringing all my scattered life lessons together...

...an extension of Silently Noisy

JAGRUTI MISTRY

INDIA • SINGAPORE • MALAYSIA

ISBN 979-8-89277-321-8

Dedication

Numerous experiences have enriched my life, and I consider myself uniquely blessed to be surrounded by amazing people, a true reflection of divine placement. In recounting my journey, I must acknowledge a few archangels who played crucial roles.

My parents, ***Pushpa Mistry and Ramchandra Mistry***, will always top this list, surpassing even the God I worship, for they introduced me to the Almighty. They have sculpted my existence, enabling me to represent myself to the best of my abilities. My mother, an unwavering source of encouragement, instilled confidence in me for every attempt, even when hesitation dawdled. My father, a man of few words, has spoken volumes through his actions, teaching me the values of genuineness, morality, and righteousness. Undoubtedly, they have been my best choices in people, and my love for them is unconditional.

In life, they say we encounter an idol we worship once, and ironically, that person embodies everything we believe about the divine. ***Vipul Patel***, affectionately addressed as Vipulbhai, is one such individual who unexpectedly altered the course of my life. Ever since that transformative moment, my life has never been the same. I am eternally grateful for the lessons learned, values imbibed, and unwavering support received. He is a blessing, and I humbly acknowledge that this was the work of a higher power.

Embarking on a journey into the unfamiliar, one often is in constant search of a guiding force—a light that provides direction in the initial stages of your career. For me, that guiding force was Nankishorji, ***Nandkishor Rankawat***. Without his mentorship in the early days of my career, I wouldn't have navigated the competitive world with such fearlessness. I am truly grateful for the lessons on making confident decisions that he imparted.

My friends and acquaintances have been the choicest blessings of the universe. I truly am a blessed child.

Speaking of children - how can I forget to mention ***my little angel, my darling niece, Prisha Matondkar,*** a powerhouse of everything, a source of boundless joy and unconditional expression of love that carries the power of brightening our day. My affection for her goes beyond what I can express, and I find myself loving her more than I even realize. I wish her a life always filled with blessings. Stay blessed always, ***Chickoo***! (as I affectionately call her).

Last but certainly not least, our ***youngest joy in the house my nephew, Hriyansh Mistry.*** As time swiftly passes, it's incredible to witness his rapid growth. I find myself continually getting to know this unique little personality. Your Coco (as he affectionately addresses me) wants you to know that your well-being means the world to me. May you always find happiness and blessings in abundance. Love to both my cherished little munchkins; you bring immeasurable joy to my heart.

Contents

Introduction

This marks the completion of my second book, and I am genuinely glad that I persevered in my writing journey. This process has not only deepened my understanding of myself but has also unveiled aspects of my identity that were previously unknown to me.

I frequently find comfort in my own world, although it's crucial to clarify that I am not an introvert. While I am outgoing and enjoy lively conversations with those I hold dear, I prefer being of more reserved conduct around unfamiliar individuals.

I have dedicated nearly two decades to the healthcare marketing field, the onset of pandemic prompted me to lean towards my creative side. After publishing my first book, I ventured into the world of podcasting on Spotify and audaciously shared my amateur singing on YouTube. The experience has been immensely enjoyable.

The act of translating thoughts onto paper has consistently proven to be a rewarding attempt for me. Throughout my writing journey, I've engaged in profound conversations with my thoughts, treating them as a sincere best friend. The progress is evident, and I find myself improving every day. My intention is to sustain this relationship for a lifetime and, moreover, to share the profound insights from these conversations with you.

Jagruti Mistry

Preface

The Abstract

Bringing all my scattered life lessons together...

Life is all about big and small instances, however while we are oblivious in those times we only realize the lessons much ahead in life. These amazing learnings surface in isolation.

I have tried my best to pen these learnings and instances; and as I did so, I re-lived these times literally almost as if walking through the scenes portrayed in movies. This second book was an experience I didn't know I needed. I am very excited about you being a part of this walkthrough and I hope you enjoy as much as I did articulating it.

I will leave you with a thought..

When you find yourself with a thought that you most hesitate to implement, I urge you to start immediately, cuz that actually may be your true calling.

Happy reading!

1. Why Am I the Way I Am

Sometimes, I come to the realization that my understanding of myself is more like viewing myself as a third person. What I do, think, and learn often remains an experience I may not always wish to share. To the outside world, I present a different persona, and I owe this unique perspective to the third person within me, the silent keeper of secrets.

It took me a while to grasp that I was actively observing my surroundings and documenting my observations. One day, I sat down and put these reflections onto paper.

Navigating through life's challenges may not be easy for everyone, but it becomes evident as we gain awareness or, to put it simply, as we age. Each person has their own way of approaching daily life and managing larger aspects. Difficult times, such as this pandemic, are a recurring theme, there will always be such challenges around; and if you scrutinize closely, everyone carries a set of worries at the forefront of their minds when they're not engaged in something exciting. Therefore, shouldn't our focus be on doing things that truly excite us rather than allowing worry to take priority?

There were moments when I questioned whether I was good enough for others or if there was more to learn from life. Interestingly, this curiosity only fueled my excitement about the unknown that lay ahead.

While I find myself having an internal commentary on everything, I prefer to keep those thoughts to myself—not out of fear of judgment but because I want to avoid cross-questioning by others. It might be too challenging for people to comprehend me (maybe). However, being comfortable with my own company is easy for me.

I share these random thoughts with you because I want to convey that everyone may have their own set of questions. I've learned that not all answers need to be known immediately; in fact, some answers may never be needed at all. The key is to focus on our 'now,' as everything is meant to unfold in its own time.

2. Growing Up

There are moments in what we often label as our 'growing up years,' where the complexity of life events leaves us clueless, despite which we refrain from questioning ourselves. Concepts of good, bad, right, and wrong seem distant, yet certain instances evoke specific unexplainable emotions within us.

All seems well until the formal schooling starts, marking a transition from the familiar borders of our homes to an environment where we are exposed to diverse teachings. Here, we encounter behaviors that might surprise us—the reactions, responses, tones of speech, and more. It takes time for these new experiences to register and be accepted, although at times, the process can be overwhelming rather than welcoming.

Reflecting on my childhood, I am grateful for the foundations laid by a nurturing environment. I was prepped on the specifics of being a well-behaved child, cultivating good manners that seamlessly became a part of my life. Interacting with people posed no difficulty. Writing this, I recognize that early on, I acquired the ability to distance myself from individuals who ***drained my energy***, a term I now understand, although back then, I simply didn't like them without any clear reason (and I harbour no guilt about it).

The concept of ***'responsibility'*** was alien to me, even when I actually started taking up studying seriously and despite of not liking certain subjects I continued to work on understanding the content.

Looking back, I realize, until we understand that there is a word representing our action we don't really have a reference to overthink on the topic. But once you name it as ***"responsibility"***, we suddenly overthink it.

Our capacity to exaggerate situations in our minds can turn the minutest thought into a source of worry. Learning to temper our reactions can often provide a straightforward solution.

As a child, if I had a question, I'd ask my mom, and the solution was simple. Once clarified, I moved on without lingering on the same question. Today, I think ***the 'disbelief' in solutions compels us to re-question our concerns***.

It's crucial to initially believe in the solution and trust that once implemented it will lead to a favorable outcome, even if it doesn't align perfectly with our expectations. **Trust is an energy** that requires continuous investment until reciprocated. Failure to understand this leads people to stop trusting, causing a breakdown in this vital cycle.

For a child the purest form of trust is their mother and that's precisely because they've only witnessed unconditional love, we have since birth trusted her energy around us without ever doubting it. Similarly, if we direct our energies towards trusting the process and believing that everything happens for our highest good, things may drastically start shifting in a way we never expected.

3. Friendships that Came and Went

I find it fascinating that we have the ability to make friends. Just think about it – you can be chatting with complete strangers one moment, and the next, you're discussing life with them. This quality, in my opinion, is often underrated. From kindergarten days, everyone starts making friends, and that's quite endearing. Those who manage to keep the same friends since then are, I guess, the lucky ones, probably...

I say probably, because I believe that somewhere along the way, the same spark is missing as we had back then. The culprit is our choices. Over the years, we encounter numerous people and face countless choices, and somehow, our frequency of interactions with people determine the depth of the relationships we form. It's quite rare to have friends with whom we don't interact regularly but still have deep friendships. I think something is missing there, perhaps it's the heart.

There are times when, for no concrete reason, we ignore our closest friends. For example, when we are lost in thought and a close friend calls, we may not want to answer simply because we are preoccupied with our own bothersome thoughts. The irony is that we're scared to admit that we just don't feel like talking. Some people even resort to lying, claiming they were busy and couldn't talk.

Self-manipulation has become a prevalent trend today. Even the nicest person might inadvertently become manipulative and think it's acceptable because the world is. There needs to be a halt to this trend; we are becoming less heart and more strategic mind. "Be Human" is supposed to reference a positive quality, while "We're not animals" is meant to be a less favorable comparison. However, I believe animals often have a better way of life.

It's high time that we introspect and eliminate what is unnecessary from our lives. Let's at least be honest with ourselves first and then expect the same from those around us.

Over time, we've seen friends and people come and go from our lives. I understand when elders say that some people come into our lives to teach us lessons meant for our growth, and when that purpose is fulfilled, they leave.

Though there also might be a different take to this, somehow, it seems we haven't learned to maintain our relationships. We say things we're not supposed to and stay silent about issues that require serious discussion. It's these difficult conversations that ultimately make us and our relationships stronger. Maybe then, we might have lasting friendships and relationships.

4. People are Everywhere

How I am is more important than the mood of those around me because I not only have the capability to attract positive energy but also possess the ability to reflect it. Imagine a world without interactions - it's hard to fathom, right?

The necessity for communication has brought the world closer. While we strive to simplify communication even with machines, we often overlook the basics within our closest network. Our interactions with others shape who we are today. Constant learning, judgment, criticism, compliments, anger, hate, love, respect - all driven by communication. Choosing how we utilize communication is perhaps the most underrated skill. Occasionally, we come across individuals who excel in communication, leaving us in awe of their abilities.

Ultimately, everything comes down to practice. Consistency is key.

Each of us is confined to our own world within, so it's crucial to introspect and identify what we want to express. Find the right vocabulary and connect with the right people for effective communication. Not everything needs to be shared with everyone; be mindful of that. What you express becomes data that can be utilized, exploited, or ignored, therefore understanding the importance of being aware of your words is crucial. Words have value, and you must choose that value and your audience carefully.

Life teaches us in its unique way through experiences and instances. I've made mistakes in choosing the right people to be with, trusting the wrong ones, but I've learned that the beauty of learning often lies in bad experiences. Now, I go with the flow, keeping it simple. Communicate transparently without hurting sentiments. We can be empathetic and clear simultaneously, and the tone of our voice works wonders.

It has made things easier for me over time.

5. Our Values

The values an individual carries are deeply linked with their conscience. While our values shape who we are, the choices we make over time play a vital role. Some people embrace experimentation, adopting a 'let's see what happens' approach, bringing their conscience and decision-making into play.

A person with a strong conscience tends to remain true to their beliefs, resisting deviation from their principles even when faced with tempting alternatives. Some argue that circumstances can force individuals into decisions they may not want to make. However, I believe there is always a way out, and if we have genuinely committed to a certain path, we typically find a way to stick to it.

I've often found myself in situations where choices needed to be made, and one option seemed to lead down a road I didn't wish to take. I recall making difficult decisions, standing firm on my beliefs.

For example, in our corporate lives, we encounter people who try to undermine us or colleagues who envy our working style, behaving or speaking in a certain manner. In such situations, my initial instinct was to respond aggressively, but I realized that mirroring their behavior would lower me to their level, which I refused to do. Instead, I chose to be myself, addressing each situation without being rude while refusing to tolerate disrespect.

It's a challenging skill to master, but once learned, it becomes intriguing. The power of self-awareness is amazing and should never be forgotten.

The ongoing process of helping oneself grow is the greatest gift and skill we can add to our lives. There will be numerous instances where we are put to the test, and the decisions we make at those times will shape our future.

Always remember to make decisions you won't regret.

6. What You are, is Not Always What You Remain to Be

We are constantly changing, whether consciously or unconsciously. However, it's essential to be aware of where we are heading and what we are evolving into. Many of us find ourselves stuck in routine, often without realizing it. Unless something significant happens or we encounter an eye-opening situation, we may not experience our 'Happy Realization' moment.

I once found myself reminiscing with friends, saying, 'those were the days' when we were so happy in our school days. Back then, we were blissfully ignorant of life's harsh realities, friends seemed less selfish, and our fights only lasted until the next playtime after school. What changed?

Life is meant to move forward, where we create moments in our present that become memories of our past.

My primary goal is to find happiness in doing something positive each day. I'm always looking to do something different, even if the nature of the work remains the same. Also, I enjoy sharing my day and achievements with everyone—not out of arrogance, but because I'm excited to celebrate even the smallest accomplishments.

Somewhere along the way, I'm appreciating the person I am becoming, and I attribute a significant part of that to everyone who has been a part of my life. I always remember learning something valuable from each person, making this journey full of continuous growth. I haven't stopped progressing through each level, and that's what makes it exciting.

Now, I'm speaking directly to you—listen up.

"You may not have brought your awareness to the massive opportunity you have of becoming better each day. However, let me also tell you that the good part is, you know now and you can act now. It's okay to have low moments sometimes, but that shouldn't bring you to a standstill. ***We often get what we want, but we forget to ask."***

7. The Love that You Think You Deserve

We all have a so-called understanding of love, and we've experienced it from different people around us — starting with Mom, Dad, siblings, relatives, friends, partners, and spouses.

We are constantly in a love-hate relationship with love, and that's what makes it so interesting. It's funny how, at one point, we feel amazing when everything is going well, but on the slightest difficulty, we hate being in love and convince ourselves that we are happy without it.

The problem arises when we expect someone else to love us the way we want, yet we barely pamper ourselves with the love we think we deserve. Primarily, experiences of love and affection come from our parents, who, in their best capacity, treat us according to their way of parenting. Sometimes they may get annoyingly difficult, but most of the time, they are always wanting the best for us. The best part is that we may fight with them royally one moment, and the next, we are asking our mom to cook our favorite food or give us a good glass of water. All of this is love, indeed. Love is when we have our absolute right over someone, and the other allows us to do so with no hard feelings.

Not everyone who speaks to us nicely necessarily loves us; sometimes, love is situational, and when a situation changes, you may discover this bitter truth.

They say finding love isn't easy, but I feel, why find love? We don't need to find love; it finds us when we are immersed in self-love and self-growth. There is a difference between seeking and chasing. We need to focus more on seeking and unlearn chasing.

As I write this, I realize I've never put my personal thoughts on this topic out there. Today, I feel I should share. I've always run away from thinking about this in my head, keeping myself busy with other things in life. I am a very sensitive person, and I feel that when I give my attention to something or someone, it will always be 100 percent, and I will pour in whatever I have to offer to the relationship. But somewhere, I always doubted if the person I love would do the same, and that's what refrained me from meeting more people and exploring this aspect of life. Well, I did encounter and had my share of 'love,' but as I said, I gave it too much too fast (that's what I feel). Today, I think differently.

I have come to realize that everything I think I want from the ideal person may not be present in the person I choose to be with. That brought me to the concept of vibe. I believe vibes are very real and authentic; once you get a good vibe from a person, you only grow to understand that person more, and I think that slowly grows into affection and more. But because we have our preconceived notions and prerequisites, we fail to be open to people around us.

In the long run, what would only matter is how much you laugh at the same joke and how much you like to communicate with each other — the rest is a myth and our initial expectations to cross that mark when we say, 'ahhh, if there are five ticks, I don't mind talking and knowing the person.' Trust me, it's really the vibe of a person, nothing else.

Every day, we make an effort to know and understand the people we love so that we can learn from them how they want to be loved and help them learn how we want to be loved back. There is really nothing more to this simple concept. We make it so complicated.

8. The Reluctant Energy, that Keeps You Low

There are moments when your day kicks off with a heavy burden of low energy, leaving you puzzled about the reluctance to rise from bed. Despite making efforts to appear normal, the enthusiasm to engage in any activity seems absent. Even with a full day ahead and tasks awaiting, there's a lack of motivation to get up and get going.

I won't claim to fully understand the complexities of depression, and I'm not a medical professional equipped to explain it. However, one thing is clear to me: every emotion has a cause, even if it's not immediately apparent. Or, to put it differently, you might be avoiding to acknowledge that there's a probable reason behind your current emotional state.

Regardless, have you considered a solution to this situation? While I may not have experienced precisely the same circumstances, I've certainly faced moments of low energy where addressing the issue was not a priority. However, I've noticed a significant improvement when I've acknowledged my subpar emotional state, identified the reasons behind it, and addressed them proactively.

It's essential to recognize and embrace what you're feeling, even if it's unpleasant. Immediate action may not always be necessary, but lingering in that negative state for an extended period is not advisable. Allowing that feeling to become a habit is similar to addiction—initially, you immerse yourself in it, and gradually, it engulfs you without realization. So, what can be done?

Let's take responsibility for ourselves. Understand that we can't simultaneously dwell in the realm of low energy and expect things to go our way. Consistently complaining and empathizing with our situation is like living in a false belief or a bubble of self-pity. Progress requires movement. While the battle may be tough, winning remains the only option. Pushing oneself to rise and engage in a preferred activity is a transformative strategy, which can alter our focus and energy.

Every day presents to us an opportunity to work on ourselves, gradually shaping the individuals we aspire to be. No shortcuts exist; it's crucial to remember this reality, and there is never an effortless escape.

Tough situations build resilient individuals.

9. Letting Go is Difficult But Necessary

The mind is a source of everything. At times, the daily hustle and the constant consumption of information over time can overwhelm it. When the mind is momentarily less occupied with important tasks, it tends to wander. Each person is a product of their past experiences.

Developing a habit of clinging too tightly to everything can be burdensome, causing overwhelming feelings. This tendency holds us back from liberating ourselves from unwanted mind ramblings. The human mind is always active, but you have complete control over what it chooses to contemplate. However, some thoughts persist and become a primary concern if they are bothersome and hinder your daily activities. The essential question to ponder is, what is occupying your mind?

Once you identify the answer and address the troubling thought, you pinpoint the area of concern. The subsequent step involves figuring out how to let go. Shifting your focus can promptly alter your thoughts, serving as the quickest method to break free from the current thinking mode. Additionally, deliberately addressing your thoughts each day and allocating time to consciously redirect your focus will eventually empower you to master the art of letting go.

Letting go is a mechanism of embracing the new, and continuing your journey in life for fresh lessons, and fostering personal growth.

10. Experiencing the Experience

This takes me back to numerous instances that left me no choice but to put myself to the test, offering invaluable learning experiences. It made me realize that certain lessons are acquired only through first hand experiences in challenging situations.

Some of these experiences provided me with a one-on-one encounter with myself, revealing how I react to specific circumstances and what I go through. Somewhere along the journey, I've forgotten to truly embrace and learn from the experiences life throws my way, and that's what I want to emphasize on now.

When challenging situations left me feeling lost, I discovered that regaining composure and facing things with the belief that "there is a solution to everything" brought me ease. Witnessing things miraculously fall into place strengthened my understanding that eventually, everything aligns for the better. Maintaining faith that we are moving forward, for positive outcomes is essential.

Let's reflect on situations we perceived as unfavorable but turned out to be the best lessons or major turning points in our lives. I've learned to be open to life, and consciously accepting everything as is while actively working towards what I desire. Acknowledging that not everything unfolds as planned, yet everything happens for the best, is a belief I wholeheartedly embrace. I refrain from questioning the master plan, as it has never failed me.

Another aspect that fascinates me is the significance of receiving. Despite our inclination towards selfless gestures, there's an equal need to be open to receiving such gestures. For instance, if you're unwell while traveling in public transport and an elderly person notices, offering their seat. In such a scenario, you may feel awkward accepting the help, but sometimes it's essential to let go of preconceived norms, express gratitude, and move forward. Receiving may initially place us in an uncomfortable position, but with an open mindset, the experience brings a sense of calmness, similar to the satisfaction we feel when extending help to others. Let's attempt to view it from a different perspective, and upon doing so, you'd discover that it hits different.

11. Meditation is Underrated

Before I probe into this topic, I want to clarify that my understanding of meditation is purely personal, and I have not undergone any formal training nor adhered to a specific technique.

My introduction to meditation occurred during my yoga classes, where, although meditation techniques weren't explicitly taught, the practice of "Shavasana" left me feeling calmer after intense training sessions. During this time, I discovered that closing my eyes allowed me to observe my thoughts as they flowed. I could witness them from a third-person perspective, gaining insight into my own thinking that I had never addressed before.

I began sitting with closed eyes, relishing the tranquility of my focused state. What started as a 5-minute meditation gradually extended to 45 minutes, with half an hour dedicated to building focus. Now, it takes me a mere 5 minutes to gather myself and focus. The transformative journey was truly remarkable—I started understanding myself better, aligning with my goals, and effortlessly ignoring distractions. It felt nothing short of magical.

While I appreciate hearing about others' meditation experiences, I am deeply in love with the personal revelations that surface during my one-on-one meditation sessions. Being present in the moment and understanding the workings of my mind is an invaluable aspect of self-discovery. Somehow, I feel more intuitive. Aligning with your thoughts makes you more aware of your energy and the energies around you, I think.

I share this in the hope that, amidst of the search for external knowledge, we remember that answers often lie within us. Patience is crucial as we wait for these revelations to unfold. Everything arrives at the right time, precisely when we need it the most.

Certainly, I still have moments of agitation and overthinking, but the ability to redirect my focus back to a calm state is an incredible skill. I encourage you to take a moment, sit down, and observe—watch what you think, and be amazed by the natural flow of thoughts.

12. Don't Get Consumed by Your Thoughts

Thoughts can be remarkably influential; it baffles me how much power I've given them, to the extent that they make me lose sight of my priorities. Regardless of the quality of these thoughts—whether they are positive or negative—I am presently more concerned with their impact on us.

There have been instances when I'd start pondering, constructing an elaborate story in my head. As one thought led to another, I gradually realized that I had fabricated more problems in my mind than actually existed. This realization had a significant effect on me.

Indeed, thoughts do have an influence on us. Since we make them feel real, they possess the capability to alter our energies.

When you catch yourself lost in thought, pay close attention to the content—what you are thinking about—and, if possible, recognize the root cause of that thought. It's not imperative to take any immediate action after identifying the cause; the goal is to become aware of our thinking patterns.

As I started to be more conscious of my thoughts, I discovered that I could exercise a significant degree of control over them. It required practice, but I made a conscious decision to work on it, and that made all the difference.

What often goes unnoticed is that our mood is intricately tied to how we feel, and our thoughts play a pivotal role in determining those feelings. Consequently, it becomes essential to monitor and regulate our thoughts.

It's crucial to remember that not every thought consumes us or steers us toward negativity. What we should strive for is thoughtful and controlled thinking.

13. EGO

Such a massive three-letter word, yet its impact is even more significant. I candidly admit that it's taken me a while to recognize and acknowledge my ego. No, I did not accept it with a pinch of salt; it was a rather subtle realization.

Ego is an emotion, and everyone's level of ego would differ depending on the situation and the people involved. Sometimes, even when you know you are reacting unnecessarily, it becomes difficult to take corrective action because our ego is mightier than the situation. It often causes more harm to ourselves than anyone around us. But in some situations it burns our surroundings like wildfire with no fault of theirs.

In such situations, I choose to keep quiet. Yes, it is challenging to stay calm in the spur of the moment, but trust me, composure allows us to think wisely.

It's important to acknowledge that having an ego is not inherently negative; instead, the key lies in effectively managing and balancing it. There is a very thin line between self-respect and ego, and one should know how to draw that line.

Certain situations necessitate a holistic approach, and that's when, despite your ego, you need to act keeping in mind the larger objective. We influence our surroundings more than we know already and therefore we need to be mindful of our actions. While ego is known to mess with our minds massively stopping us from being considerate of others.

We therefore need to take a step back to understand and respond, rather than reacting immediately.

14. Stuck in a Thought of Finding a Perfect Career

Time is ticking" is a so called bitter truth that often crosses our mind when we are in a haste or not enjoying what we are currently at. Those who are truly enjoying life seldom bother to check the time.

Every day, people follow their planned routines or navigate through unplanned, monotonous ones. In essence, life becomes a series of routines. Reflecting on my personal experiences, I've had moments of realization. During my early workdays, amidst a busy schedule, I often pondered the future of my current ventures. However, I found myself stuck in a loop of uncertainty, unable to find clear answers about what to do next.

My perspective has since evolved. I now have a clearer vision of my goals, allowing me to work gradually without questioning my current circumstances. I dedicate my time and effort wholeheartedly. This shift in mindset has transformed the way I perceive challenges; I no longer complain about my situation or doubt the journey ahead.

We all tend to overanalyze our thoughts, creating mental clutter that can lead to frustration and anxiety. Taking some 'me time' can be immensely beneficial, though it requires a daily effort. Personally, I've discovered a profound sense of peace and calmness by practicing this simple task—spending time alone and observing my thoughts.

Work will always demand our attention, but it's crucial for us to decide how much we allow it to consume us. Finding joy in the daily aspects of life is a personal choice. Self-awareness is underrated, when one discovers what one can find just by being self-aware, a lot will change.

15. Self-Love

You are the right person in the perfect body, and that's the most beautiful thing that has ever happened to you, period! Let me be honest—I wasn't even aware of this concept, and I suspect many others aren't either. The exact meaning of this idea might elude many. However, I've been introduced to it in recent years, and trust me, I am paving my own path to understand its essence. For me, it is an endless journey.

Upon discovering the term 'Self-Love,' I was pleasantly surprised. Additionally, the phrase 'Main apni favorite hoon,' translating to 'I am my own favorite' in English, caught my attention in a Bollywood movie. I was captivated by this concept and began fostering self-awareness—acknowledging my qualities, contemplating the changes I desired, and more. Unknowingly, I had innately imbibed a sense of self-love even before encountering this concept, perhaps a trait typical of Gemini, I guess.

Self-love encompasses taking care of oneself, thinking freely, pursuing activities that ignite passion, understanding one's mental struggles, safeguarding mental peace from external influences, believing in oneself against all odds, and respecting oneself even during self-talk. It involves walking away from anything that compromises your self-respect, growth, mental health; and also involves recognizing your boundaries, and ensuring others are aware of them. All these aspects collectively define self-love.

When you love yourself, you naturally extend that love to others and treat them with respect.

Teach yourself to give time and attention to the only person who cries first when hurt.

16. If You Think You are Unimportant, Check Again

Many assert that we are mere specks in an immense universe, suggesting our existence might be inconsequential. However, consider this: just as every drop of water contributes to the depth of the ocean, without you something major would have been missing in this grand tapestry of existence.

Somewhere, somehow, something changed because you exist. Someone's day may be brighter, circumstances may have shifted, all simply because of your presence. This, my friend, is one of the profound reasons for your existence.

Looking at the intricacies of life, I am astonished at the meticulousness of the creator. Each person is navigating their unique journey, yet there is an incredible sense of order, not a speck out of place. How can we not aspire to contribute to this life and create a beautiful outcome?

My personal aspiration is to create something meaningful, making a positive impact on as many lives as possible. The thought of finding ways to help others, sharing my knowledge, and making a difference keeps me excited and motivated.

Consider the possibility that our primary purpose here is to contribute to the greater good, yet we often find ourselves entangled in insignificant matters such as relationships, money, careers, and the so-called rat race. Life transcends these aspects; allow yourself moments of introspection and retrospection. In doing so, you may find peace in understanding yourself, making the complexities of life appear simpler.

17. Our Perceptions

What we perceive about a person or situation may not always be accurate. It's crucial to recognize that relying solely on our own perceptions can lead to misunderstandings. Instead, engaging in meaningful conversations when necessary and asking the right questions can provide relevant answers, bringing clarity and composure to the mind.

Personally, I've struggled with overthinking, leading to unnecessary mental turmoil and unresolved resentments. I've come to understand that there is always another side to the story, one that requires careful consideration and a calm mindset.

A calm mind allows us to view things through a neutral lens, changing the way we perceive situations. Our diverse perspectives stem from individual thinking patterns. At times, we may magnify simple situations into grave problems within our minds, when in reality, they are hardly worth the worry.

We can break free from these mental chaos by interrupting the build-up of situations in our minds. Changing our focus, perhaps by stepping back and observing the situation as a third person, can make a significant difference. Providing our minds with respite from unnecessary clutter is essential to prevent our brains from carrying unnecessary burdens.

While it's easier said than done, consistent practice is the key to achieving these mental shifts. At times, we hold onto situations and people so tightly that we inadvertently impose more harm upon ourselves than necessary. Learning to maintain a healthy distance from everything around us is a valuable lesson, although perfection is not the primary focus. It's through effort and continuous practice that we can refine our mental chatter and strive for improvement.

18. Fix Your Mind

Everything you engage in involves your mind—your reactions, responses, behavior, anxiety, and mood. The foremost aspect to address while working on oneself is the mind. Now, the question arises: does the mind play games? Well, the mind is like a child—it may exhibit behaviors we wish to avoid, yet it continues to wander like a mischievous brat that chooses to ignore. Acting as a mindful parent is the key, handling it with care, mindfulness and vigilant observation of your thoughts play a very important role in gaining a deeper understanding of your mind.

In various situations, I've found myself to be an overthinker, with my mind operating at lightning speed. Managing my thoughts was once a daunting task, but gradually, I learned to observe and guide my mind intentionally. It wasn't a swift journey; rather, it demanded practice and patience. There were moments when I sat down, acknowledged my thoughts, and logically made peace with them. While I agreed to disagree at times, I never disagreed to agree.

My go-to solution involves delving into the thoughts racing through my mind, understanding their origins, and reasoning with them. Another effective approach is articulating the thoughts in detail, a method that aids in tackling and processing them.

The mind has a tendency to keep one occupied, you need to develop a stronger muscle in your brain to prevent it from dictating and controlling one's actions.

A somewhat unconventional yet effective approach involves engaging in a conversation with your mind. Trust me, it's one of the most beneficial things you can do for your mental well-being. Having a dialogue with your mind, understanding the reasons behind distress, and actively working towards resolution can yield profound results.

19. Dealing with a Loss

Losing someone creates a void in our hearts and minds that is challenging to articulate. Coping with such a situation is deeply personal, and navigating the emotions that accompany grief can be overwhelming.

Our connections with those in our lives, whether loved ones, close family, or those with whom we share a unique bond, become integral parts of our existence. When we realize they are no longer present, it shatters the hope of their physical proximity, a pain that cannot be put into words.

Despite the difficulty, life must persist, as the undeniable truth remains – we are still here.

In the face of numerous questions, the foremost challenge is often figuring out what to do next and finding the motivation to continue the journey. I believe, above all else, we need to allow ourselves to grieve in our own way. Some express their sorrow vocally, some retreat into self-reflection, while others confide in those closest to them. Regardless of your approach, take the time to grieve, acknowledging that it is a process of releasing emotions, not sinking into despair.

Surrounding yourself with supportive individuals, redirecting your focus to work, and taking breaks to check in with yourself are essential coping mechanisms. It's okay to feel low, experience sadness, and entertain thoughts - we are human beings with complex emotions.

Emotions are meant to be felt and expressed; find your way to do so genuinely and thoroughly. Time, often hailed as the best healer, has an inherent ability to mend wounds. Allow yourself the freedom to express without restriction, as suppressing emotions can lead to unexpected eruptions.

Through the journey of self-healing, you emerge as a stronger individual. ***Always remember one crucial thing - when you feel the need, always speak!***

20. Testing Situations

I don't know how many of you get scared of exams, but as a child, I was genuinely terrified of them. Looking back, I wish someone sat me down to explain that life is primarily about learning and overcoming every test to progress. Unfortunately, certain crucial realities of life aren't explicitly taught to us.

Introspection often leads to profound self-realizations and revelations, not to shock us but to help us comprehend that things unfold as they are supposed to, contributing to our growth and transformation into beautiful beings.

Have you ever found yourself feeling overwhelmed by a situation? Sometimes, it feels like an intense cardiac arrest, and the most challenging part is the inability to change it.

So, what does one do when in such a space?

The answer is often nothing. In situations where finding a logical solution seems impossible, we are meant to undergo these experiences. As the saying goes, 'Time heals everything.' While it may sound cliché, it holds true. Time moves swiftly, especially when you choose to accept and move forward. Those who linger in a situation for an extended period may find themselves feeling stuck.

Certainly, there are sensitive situations where shifting focus is challenging. During such times, being with ourselves is crucial to understanding and acknowledging the pain. Once we embrace the pain, dealing with it becomes more manageable.

The beauty of life lies in its constant movement, unfolding surprises and presenting choices before us. Much like a game of cricket, you get to decide how to play each ball thrown your way. Remember, tough times are momentary—they don't last.

21. Commitment is Everything

For me, commitment embodies loyalty to myself and my decisions. It required considerable introspection and determination to sit down and reconcile with how this concept should align with my values and make sense for my personal growth.

Procrastination used to be a significant hurdle in my life, primarily due to a lack of consistency. Incorporating the term 'loyalty' into my commitment transformed my perspective, creating a sense of responsibility within me.

Loyalty is a word that can have an impact on your conscience and that's why; when you relate commitment and loyalty it kind of compels you and pushes you to stick to your decisions.

I appreciate the power of a simple hack in self-development. Well, everyone has their unique approach to self-discipline.

The mind, akin to a child, can be influenced and guided to understand certain concepts. The phrase 'Mind plays games' is familiar, but you can turn the tables and use it to your advantage. If you feel unprepared for substantial commitments in your routine, start with smaller ones:

- Reflect on what forces you to deviate from sticking to a routine.
- Identify tasks you dislike, as understanding your aversions allows you to explore alternative options.
- Challenge yourself to maintain consistency for a week and observe the resulting motivation.
- Acknowledge that every time you push yourself to complete a challenging task, you are building your mental resilience.

Commitment is everything, it pushes you towards your goals while simultaneously helping you overcome reservations and obstacles.

Be loyal to what you commit to yourself!

22. Feelings are Extraordinary

Certain life experiences elicit profound responses and sensations, often challenging us to understand what's going on. However, I want to assure you that you are not alone in this struggle.

In those intense moments, it becomes crucial to manage oneself. Post-reflection, there is a deep realization that evolves into a valuable lesson. We often rush through situations and emotions, neglecting to fully comprehend the depth of our emotional responses.

Life, with its intense highs and lows, presents to us moments where questions overflow, but answers remain elusive. However, here's the silver lining: ***answers aren't always necessary.*** More often than not, the essence lies in navigating through the experience itself.

What I've come to understand is that things start falling into place when you allow yourself to calm down and simply be—with the pain, the void, and the anxiousness. Embracing these emotions fully leads to a crucial moment where you confront the feeling head-on. This journey culminates in acceptance, realization, lessons learned, and a clear understanding of what action needs to be taken.

Surprisingly, profound wisdom often stems from within, but it requires us to endure life's toughest challenges.

This, my friend, is what we refer to as paying the price. Nothing worthwhile comes effortlessly, but with time and experience, you can transform the seemingly challenging into something manageable.

Wisdom, as it turns out, is a costly pursuit. It leaves scars, breaks you, but in the end, it molds you into a better version of yourself.

23. This is Me Talking to Me

How I wish the world knew more about the realm you belong to. The depth of your intricate thoughts is yet to be unveiled because each expression hints at a journey that has infinite layers to unfold, indicating the path ahead is vast and nuanced.

Within you are oceans of caged secrets protected by the bars of your heart waiting for a storm to reveal them all, but yet you appear a calm sea that finds contentment in the stillness of your own depths.

Often, you dive in to conceal your wounds to cry aloud in silence, in a space unknown to none.

No, you are not aware of what's happening in the territories of the world, but you surely have reached vacuums no one has been.

I know the vastness of your mind that harbors dreams humongous as the skies, but again, you chose a slow deliberate pace focused on every step you take knowing one day it will be no less than a curtain raise.

I admire the way you've humbled down aware of everything around, but one day I know an eye will look through your soul and find one's peace within you, that day the sea will make friends with the shore like never before.

www.ingramcontent.com/pod-product-compliance
Lightning Source LLC
LaVergne TN
LVHW091237150826
845673LV00003B/1191

* 9 7 9 8 8 9 2 7 7 3 2 1 8 *